Bouquets

Letting Them Go

Alfa

Copyright © 2018 Alfa
Editor: Ashley Jane
Main Illustrator: Angie Shea
(full art credits on page 100)

Alfa Holden
Kentucky, USA
WWW.ALFAPOET.COM

Bouquets: Letting Them Go/
Alfa Holden 2nd Edition
ISBN 978-0-9980503-3-1

Contents

Notes on the Author

There are very few contemporary poets who have mastered the ability to weave emotions into their work as vividly and authentically as Alfa does. She has a gift, and anyone who has ever read her work has felt the warmth of it. Her poetry and prose unearth the feelings and the fears we try to bury and gives them back to us with love and permission to let them go again - this time, with grace. Alfa is a treasure and her work is timeless, and I know it will remain in the hearts and on the bookshelves of poetry lovers long after she is gone.
- Nicole Lyons, author of The Lithium Chronicles

Alfa's poetry is a beautiful weaving of words and feelings. Her work is exquisite. From the moment you open one of her collections, you are immersed in a world of emotion. There is a wonderful journey to every facet of life in all her wonderful books.
- Cheryl Churchill, author of Petals of the Moon

Alfa has the softness of a southern lady holding your hand as she explains life's little nuances. Behind the smile is a warrior with a spine of steel born of tears and pain. Her poetry offers words of wisdom to heal and nourish her readers.
- Gypsy Mercer, author of Into the Fire

Alfa is an incredible person and writer. Nobody pens survival, love, and the overall emotion of the human experience, like she does. Her words are a gift that everyone should hold in their hands and hearts.

- Tiffany Aurora, author of The Wild Keeps Her Holy

Alfa is warmth in its purest form. She radiates kindness and goodness in a way we seldom see anymore, and her poetry reflects that. Even in moments that would tear most of us apart, she pushes through: a survivor, a warrior, a giver. She places little pieces of herself in every poem. Her heart beats on the page, and her soul shines in every line. She writes of love and heartache, and how both are vital to our growth. She guides her readers down a road of understanding, of learning when to hold on and when to let go. She has lived the pain, and now, she shares the wisdom from all those lessons learned.

- Ashley Jane, author of All Darkness and Dahlias

Alfa is not only one of the kindest souls, but such an amazingly gifted writer. Her words flow from one page onto the next. Each piece she shares with the world is another piece for my heart to connect with.

- Jessie Michelle, author of Conversations with the Moonlight

Alfa

Conveyer Belt

Life is in fact always moving
like a conveyer belt... and fast.
People move in and out of your life
like the line at the grocery store.
Here today, gone tomorrow.
You learn to try new items
when your favorites
have been discontinued.
And every time you swallow
the foreign taste,
you remember the one
your heart truly loved,
and you get nostalgic
for a slower time.
One without self-checkout.

She Isn't Really Gone

Sometimes when I look in your eyes,
I see the person I used to be.
I see the silhouette
of the person you fell in love with.
I watch her, her movements so fluid.
I feel her, her vibrancy.
And for a second,
I feel the surge fist under my ribs.
The hope blossoms into beauty,
and I think I can be her... again,

and maybe she isn't really gone.

Questioning

How many

  questions

    do you

      carry around

       because the

        answers

         have never

          held weight?

Inspiration

When you tell me *I am inspiring,*
I feel like such a fake.
Because if I told you
that I had to
force myself to write,
just to inspire MYSELF
to keep going...
would it make you
think less of me?

Silence

Silence doesn't make
your love
G
  R
    O
      W.

It makes you question
its existence.

Clueless

There are days
I cannot get out
of bed.
I communicate
solely from my phone
with the same emojis
and plentiful hearts
I usually do
to let you know
I care,
and the world

has no idea.

Feelings

Can you do me
the honor
of not
disregarding
my feelings?

Strike Out

I'm left to wonder
how the parts of me
you used to admire
are the reasons
you give for leaving.
How does one embrace
uniqueness
and then throw it
in your face?
Why step up
to the plate,
if you are not
even going to swing?

Silent Thunderstorm

I am as gentle
as a thunderstorm,
silent as lightning.
And I feel...
I feel every breath

the Universe breathes.

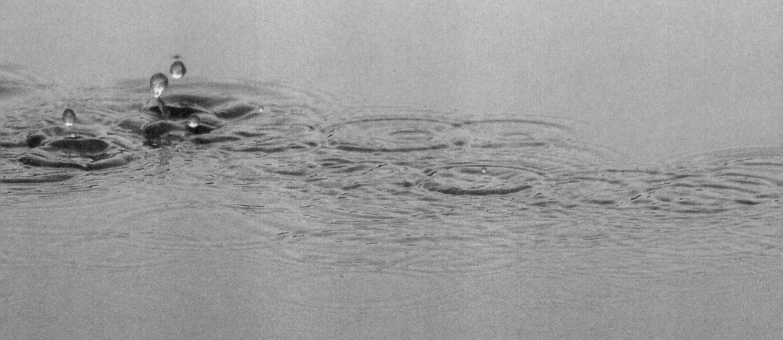

Raindrops

When the rain pelts,
I feel every drop.
And I plead...
the secrets that keep
my house
much too full,
will wash away
in the gutter.

Prada

I

wear

strength

like

you

wear

Prada.

Bullies

I would like to remind those who try
to hold my head down low
and force me to do their bidding...

I BITE.

Agreeable

It goes without saying

that agreeing with popular beliefs

is the easiest road to take.

It's the easiest to agree with

because thought process is not required.

It's the easiest to voice because no words are needed.

Your compliant nod will suffice.

Going the popular route

is always the easiest for most

– unless you have an authentic soul.

Then you speak up.

Then you become complicated.

Then you become unpopular.

Stay unpopular.

Worthiness

Your worth as a person
is not defined
by your job,
how much you earn,
or what social circles
you surround yourself with.
Your worth as a person
is determined
by the value
you place on hearts...

including your own.

Grace

Watch how a Weeping Willow
handles the seasons.
She is grace
in every condition.

Clouds

Black clouds don't always mean despair.
Sometimes they foretell a cleansing -
an upcoming storm.
And with each labored drop,
you will wash yesterday away.

Invitation

If you invite me in
to your hidden rooms,
I promise not to take
such a gesture
for granted.

Understanding

And even
if at the end
of the day
you cannot
understand
the madness,
your willingness
to try
makes me feel
understood.

Cocoon

All my hope
was bound in a
cocoon of silk wrapped
prayers.
And as my ribcage
released the hurt
and forgiveness,
my soul emerged
with wings.

Homecoming

I will always burn for you
with a light that is forever on
in anticipation
of your homecoming.

Focus

I will focus
on the light
and let it lead
my wandering heart
through the canopies
of regret.

My Story

In the past, I have been guilty of fixating

on every negative thing that came my way.

I let things that didn't deserve a minute of my time,

overshadow the blessings I took for granted.

When I made the switch to start focusing on the good,

rather than the bad, my quality of life went through the roof.

One small change led to another, and then another.

I discovered parts of myself I had neglected.

Most importantly - SELF-LOVE.

The anger I harbored eased.

Empathy grew.

But the remarkable part about positivity

is the effect it had on my heart and soul.

For the first time in my life, I feel like we are on the same page...

and I am excited to be a part of my story.

Hopeful Heart

My mind is spectacularly persuasive at night.

Whatever I valiantly battled

during the day

is pushed to the empty side

of my bed

as my mind

encourages

my spine to relax.

My hands to unfurl.

My heart to hope

that tonight...

tonight is the night

you realize

the distance is too far

and that nothing else

matters more

than filling the empty spot

at home.

Saving Our Energy

Feelings aren't disposable you know.
I wait in the wings while I watch you fly
amidst the painted skies.

The hue is too blue,
and the clouds are held tight
by imaginary support,
but still, you are easily
ensnared by the beauty of it all.

Life shouldn't be about
making public niceties.

We become accessories
to their inflated egos.
We help them frost their cakes
with icing that is much too sweet
for the real world.

We are the pawns
in their games
of mental warfare.

We should focus more
on loyalty to the people
who don't use others
for their personal gain,
but instead,

want only friendship.

I Only Need the Ocean Within Me

I swam in your depths,

thinking I could find me.

But when I came up

for air,

I realized

I have always

been a mermaid

searching for love

among dry souls.

You've Got to Let Them Go

I promised myself for years

that I would let the past go

and embrace my future.

It took many of these

broken promises

before I was able

to forgive myself

for holding on to memories

that I could conjure out of thin air.

But once I replaced the longing

of *past love*

with *present day love,*

I realized the person

I was missing

was me.

Valuable Lessons

If you think you have seen
the last of heartache,
think again.
The difference is that next time
you will have an arsenal of experience
at your disposal.
It doesn't make the pain LESS,

but it is bearable.

B a r e l y.

You know you can get through.
Sometimes that knowledge
is the thread of hope
that you grasp tightly to,
and... you get through.
Your soul expands with
a cache of fortitude
and resilience.
And you will find true love
within the chaos of all those
lessons learned.

Winding Roads

Every winding road of my past
has led me to a scenic present.
Every place I have been has touched me
and stained me with its color.
I am a believer in change.
When I left the darkness behind,
it was then that I discovered
that beauty comes when you mesh
the *old you,*
with the *new you.*
Then and only then,
can you find
the peace
within
your soul.

Promises, Promises

All the promises
he made
sprouted wings
and followed
his taillights.

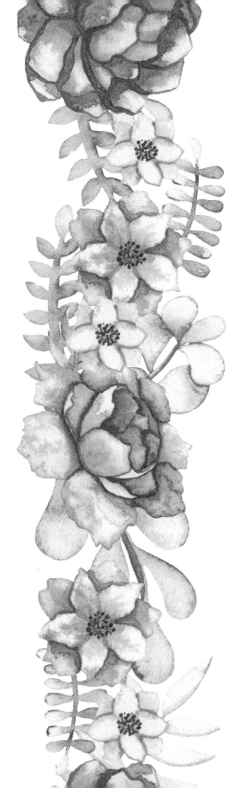

Recipe

If you let someone else decide
what you are made of,
you will never use the
ingredients that make you,
Y O U.

They want you bland
because, side by side,
it will make
what they are serving
taste better.

Add your own spice
to the world
and be *authentic*.

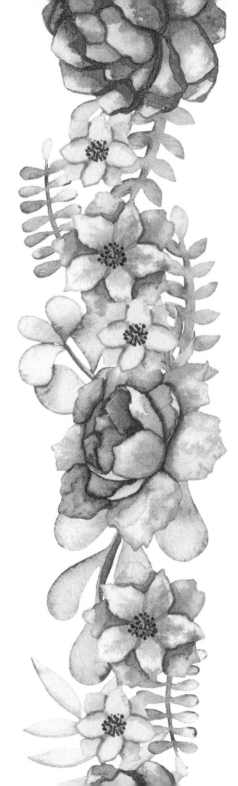

Try not to compare
yourself to others
because you will
always have something
that works in your favor:
Your talent.
Your view.
Your voice.
Your heart.

This world is hungry
FOR LOVE.

Make it. Share it.

What If?

What if I never find him?

The one who will know

how to decipher the language

my heart reserves for the special one.

What if I never find the one

who will sit and listen

for hours while I interpret

all the love stored

within my chest...

for him?

All That Remains

Your
leaving
left
cinders
and
charred
memories.

Bruised

Love is
    the bruise
      that likes
        to remind you
          of the injury.

Weighed Down

Little liar
with your head hanging low,
your shoulders give you away.
You still carry his memory.

Listen

Are you
listening
to the words
your heart
keeps hidden?
Press your ear
to its door
and learn all its
SECRETS.

Lost in the Fog

If clarity
is armor,
then surely
the fog
is his memory.

Tend to the Roots

He tried to lift
her heavy
    heavy heart,
and instead decided
to bend down,
and hold it,
leaving its roots
    firmly intact.

Long Haul Love

Are you in this for the long haul?
When my feet are spent,
will you help me stand again?
Your support means
everything to me.

Roar

She is silent when angry.
She likes to process the hurt
before she speaks openly.
But sometimes,
the words
will not come.
So, she searches for
a secluded alcove,
and she lets
her heart

ROAR

Culprit

We are all seeking the same thing
in one way or another.
We are either chasing love
or running away from love.
But love is always involved.

Static in the Line

Hearts connect,
but they do not always
communicate.
Hence, the disconnection.

Revealed

It is hard to love
with every fiber of yourself.
You undress your soul,
and you reveal the parts
you have laboriously tried to guard.
You are never more naked
than when you tell someone
how you really feel.
You peel your inhibitions back.
You shed your winter coat
and pray that you will
feel sunshine.

Life Sentence

I am always tangled
in strands of yesterday,
trussed and bound
in memories that refuse
to let me breathe.
They hold me prisoner
without a fair trial.
But I am already doing
a life sentence.
My heart will forever
hold me accountable
for our demise.

The Lies We Tell Ourselves

I tell myself that I cannot miss
what I have never had.
That is how I deal with the void
that stretches in my heart.
That is how I address the questions.
Sometimes the *not knowing*
is the blanket
that will warm your soul.

That Isn't Love

And if he lifts a hand to hurt,

instead of to help,

there is NEVER

a justification

for his behavior.

There is NEVER

an excuse.

He should NEVER

be given a free pass.

You do not need those arms

holding you tonight

when they will hurt you

tomorrow.

Deserve

You didn't deserve
the treatment you endured.
No matter how many
reasons,
excuses,
or justifications
are given to you,
you didn't deserve it.

Never Ever Settle

He called me foolish
because I wanted love.
He was willing to settle
for its absence.
And I could not
settle at all.

They
warned
me
about
you.

Afraid

Are you afraid of me

because you know I am capable

of loving the memory of you

just as much

as the presence of you?

The End

I'll probably be the only
regret you will remember
as your days draw closer
to the end.

Impassable Terrain

Whenever I think of him
I picture a mile-wide chasm.
Impassable terrain.
I think of everything
that keeps us apart.

Then he walks in the room
and the landscape
FADES AWAY.

And I forget all the reasons
why he should not be here.

They Come for Me at Night

They come for me at night.
I feel their all consuming
presence as they enter
my space and share my bed.
My room is filled
with soft breathing
and the sounds of owls
celebrating the darkness.
Feathery caresses begin
their transit up and down
the nape of my neck,
and my mind is clay
in the hands of its maker.
They come for me at night.
Always... Memories of you.

Invasion

I breathed,
and I felt his judgement
enter my safe space.
I knew my freedom
was in jeopardy.
My life depended upon
me handling the invasion
swiftly, and with finality.
I exhaled,

and let him go.

I looked over your shoulder and saw the trail of broken hearts you left behind, but I believed the excuses you gave for their dire straits. Now I am lying amongst the wreckage, labeled a crazy one, trying to make eye contact with your new arm candy. She has the same look of pity as she stares back, just like I once did. And I know she will never believe the truth from crazy lips. So, I ready a place to cushion her fall, and I whisper, *"See you soon."*

Tree Circles

You will see him again

after the trees have circled

20 years on the calendar,

and you will realize

that your life would not be what it is

had you circled life with him.

Sometimes the seasons we miss the most

are fairytale fueled nostalgia.

They aren't based on reality

but on our inability to quiet hearts

who cannot handle losing.

Live and Let Go

Until you let the past go,
you will never be free to fly.
And there is so much out there
that your precious heart
needs to see.

Learning

I learned something today.
I learned that I am guilty
of wasting a majority
of my precious minutes
focusing and dwelling
on things that are out
of my control.
I cannot ever get that
time back, but I can resolve
not to act so reckless
with the gift
of my life,
again.

I Tried

I hope
they
remember
that I tried
to make
that dash
breathe.

Dwelling

I think
what bothers us the most
is that we may not have the strength
tomorrow,
to handle the pain we feel
right now.

It doesn't matter what you do or say,
they will think you are crucifying them.
Some people hold themselves in such
high regard that they will wrongly assume
the entire world is talking about them.
Every meme and status on social media
will be critiqued and skewed until they
find a part of themselves somewhere
between the lines.
It's how they validate their importance.

Remember This

When they ambush you,
and they will,
always remember
that they'll
try to tear down
what they were
too lazy
to build
for themselves.

Envy

Every time you take a shot
meant to bring me down,
it is a reminder
that I possess
something you covet.
And you smolder hate.
You waste precious energy
trying to extinguish
what you are incapable
of igniting.

list of names:

Karma

Let's teach them

that being kind doesn't

ensure the world

will always

reciprocate.

But it will

ensure that karma

will take note.

Beat Down

The people who hurt you

trained your spirit

to expect to be

beat down.

We must retrain

ourselves so

our self-worth

will defy this role.

Authenticity

She seemed to encounter those that spent an exorbitant
amount of time ensuring that she viewed them
different than the rest. They always set out to make
themselves unique and unforgettable.
She never knew if they were authentic
or practicing for a casting call.

Solid

We cannot expect another person to fix our problems.

Well back that up...we can expect them to,

but that's a backward step in the midst of your healing process.

We need to deal with our own life bombs.

(You know, when the Universe is out of whack,

and it has a homing device velcroed to your forehead.)

But...and this is a huge but...

having someone in your life that does not cower and run,

but stays by your side, ready to aid you in any way possible,

is a showmanship of true love.

Not to mention it highlights their true character.

It's Due

Little girl

with a heart

so blue.

Open your eyes

to love again.

It's due.

First Love

When you are touched deeply by love as a child,

you spend the rest of your days trying to recreate the awakening of your heart.

And if you're lucky, you find a love that fits into the curve of that memory.

The kind of love that doesn't possess a yawn

and doesn't need an alarm clock to keep it motivated day after day.

The Quiet Ones

Just because you're quiet and don't react to every pin that drops, people may assume you are unfeeling. Some of the most empathetic souls are those that do not have to tell the world how caring they are. They give with their right hand, and the left is unaware. Their personal boundaries stay damp because they are forever letting the unkind and untrue words of naysayer's flow past their feet - floods of hate from enemies. They do not have the energy to go fight off assumptions. These silent warriors do not call attention to themselves, so they are often overlooked or thought worthless because they are not on the battlefield screaming loud.

But they are doing their part.

Not everyone will need an army behind them to make a difference.

Some do it quietly, but their impact is E V E R L A S T I N G.

Stronger

It is the middle of the night
and you are wondering
if you can make it through.
You can.
You have been here before,
but you are stronger now,
fortified with soulful armor.
You do not bend with
every breeze.
Tomorrow is less frightening
because you conquered yesterday.
You are so much stronger
than you know.

Heartache Warriors

We are not all broken.
Some of us are
recovering heartache warriors.

We are not damsels in distress.
We know what we want,
and we know what we are *waiting* for.

Isn't sincerity what we all ache for?

Someone who does not
give up the first time
their love is questioned.

Someone who does not love
their pride more than the thought
of forever with you.

Someone who has strength
in spades,
but chooses to wield
it by a gentle hand.

You could call this person
a Warrior, or even a Viking,
but really, they are just soulful,
and believe in true love.

All Wrong

It seems something always has to be hidden
in order for something else to shine.
Friendships shouldn't be that way.
Relationships shouldn't be that way.

Love shouldn't be that way.

Not Worth the Chase

Why do you continue to keep
your heart invested when they
use you as a revolving door?
If they walk,
no matter what excuse they give,
do not chase them
with feet or with questions.
Change your number.
Burn the pictures.
Shut the door... AND BOLT IT.

Sword of Strength

I have never been prouder of you than I am today. I saw the defeat climb high in your eyes and when I thought you would succumb, you pulled out your sword of strength and swung with all your might.

And I knew I need not worry.

You will be fine.

Mourning and Rebirth

Her heart was crushed bouquets,

buried along with a soul laid to rest.

Her body was a cathedral filled with mourning.

But her resurrection was one of glory and rebirth.

Know Your Worth

My soul is worth more than the pennies you threw at it.

Breathable Skin

One day you will reach a point where you will claim ownership of yourself.

The suffocation is gone, and you inhale deeply until your lungs feel sweet and full.

Your skin will finally feel like you own it. You will feel breathable.

Choice

We can live in denial
by settling for comfortable
or we can choose
to pursue the passions
that question our existence.

It is our choice.

Rainbow Hued Eyes

Your eyes will shine again. Vibrant and rainbow hued. You will look at the world and see beauty instead of desolation. You will wash off the hands that hurt you in a waterfall of new love. You will smile again.

And it won't be forced.

Showpiece

Your heart wears its journey.
Showcase it proudly.

You've Got This

As bad as it hurts now,
would it be more bearable
if you knew its intensity
would lessen tomorrow?
Chances are the pain
will still be there,
but so will your reserve
of strength.

You

have

got

this.

Acknowledgements

Mom: I wrote this for you in 2017. I hope you like the new revised version even more!

My children and grandchildren: I'm sorry you've have had to endure my hermit status. Thank you for loving me. *I love you.*

Ashley and Angie: Thank you for all of your hard work on this book, and for your unselfish support of my passion. You always have my back and my best interests at heart, *and I am forever grateful for you both.*

Regina, I will always love you for believing in me and for your gentle nudge.

Sage Poets: Your friendship speaks for itself... *I love you all.*

To Jesus Christ. You are the reason in every season of my life. Thank you for taking me on the pathway that has led me to today.

A big thank you to my readers. This is *forever* for you!

About the Author

Alfa would paint the world in hues of turquoise if she could. Unapologetic about her realistic take on heartache, she writes to let her readers know they are not alone in their pain. Her four children and soon-to-be four granddaughters, the stars of her life, were the catalysts that pushed her to force her words and her smile on the world after a lifetime of depression and anxiety.

She is best known for sharing her writing via her Facebook pages and through her Instagram account, though you can find her across most social media platforms. Since her poetry journey began, her words have been shared countless times by celebrities, used in tattoos, and included in art. Her words have spread across countries and cultures. She was signed by St Martin's Press and Castle Point Books, and she currently has six books through them, including re-released copies of her first two books: Abandoned Breaths and Silent Squall. She will be releasing another book with them in Spring 2020.

Alfa holds degrees in English Literature as well as Radiologic Sciences. She credits her ability to express painful life experiences from studying the human body from the inside out. When not writing, she is most likely indulging in iced tea, feet up, relaxing on her wide-planked porch in Louisville, Kentucky or painting an upcycled furniture piece a fabulous shade of turquoise.

Other books by this Author.

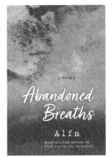

Abandoned Breaths

Silent Squall

I Find You in the Darkness

Amid Thirsty Vines

I Needed a Viking

The Salt in His Kiss

Find Me on Social Media

Web: www.alfapoet.com

Facebook: www.facebook.com/alfawrites

Instagram: @alfa.poet

Twitter: @alfa_poet

Pinterest: www.pinterest.com/alfainky

Etsy: www.etsy.com/shop/AlfaWorldwide

Tumblr: @alfa_poet

Lettrs: Alfa #539352

Art Credits:

Cover Photo: Milan Popovic
Cover Design: Samantha Haeffele/Ashley Jane

Main Illustrator: Angie Shea
Additional Illustrations by:
Nour Tahomy
Mitch Green
Marsala Digital
Anna Babich

Photography by:
Annie Spratt
Ali Abdul Rahman
Oliver Sjostrom
Hendrik Will
Ray Hennessey
Savs
Christian Grab
Oleg Magdi
Anastasiia Ostapovych
Todd Trapani
Melanie Simon

Printed in Great Britain
by Amazon

80429089R00059